LEARNING TO REVIEW

A BOOK REVIEW TRAINING MANUAL

BRED

WRITE-FOR-ME-ORGANIZATION

Copyright © SEPTEMBER 2023 WRITE-FOR-ME-ORGANIZATION

All rights reserved

The characters and events portrayed in this book are fictitious. Any similarity to real persons, living or dead, is coincidental and not intended by the author.

No part of this book may be reproduced, or stored in a retrieval system, or transmitted in any form or by any means, electronic, mechanical, photocopying, recording, or otherwise, without express written permission of the publisher.

ISBN: 9798861352369

Printed in the United States of America

BOOK REVIEW DEPARTMENT (BRED) TRAINING MANUAL

H.O.D

M.C N.U.D Olatunji

Project Coordinators

MC Dr Joshua Obasa
MC Edache Ogwuche Moses

Contributors

MC Uzezi Oyise
MC Eunice Jiwai Ibrahim
MC Okere Amara
MC Rev Dr Babatunde G Ogundunmade
MC Dr IfeOluwa Amao
MC N.U.D Olatunji
MC Dr Joshua Obasa
MC Edache Ogwuche Moses
MC Pharm. Fatima Abdulkadir

TABLE OF CONTENT

1. Introduction - What is Book Review
2. Components of a good review
3. Reading for Comprehension
4. How to identify key points
5. Summary writing
6. Common Grammatical Errors
7. Critical Thinking and Appraisal
8. Major Parts of a Book Review
9. Benefits of a Book Review

CHAPTER ONE

INTRODUCTION

What Is Book Review?

A review is a critical evaluation of a text, event, object, or phenomenon. Reviews can consider books, articles, entire genres or fields of literature, architecture, art, fashion, restaurants, policies, exhibitions, performances, and many other forms.

Book reviews are a form of literary criticism analyzing an author's ideas, writing techniques, and work quality. The analysis is opinion-based and relevant to the book's contents, making it a practice for students who want to become editors.

A book review contains a critical analysis of a book, including a narrative synopsis, information on the main characters and principal ideas, and a positive or negative assessment of the author's style of writing.

The content helps readers decide whether to grab a book or skip it by offering readers various perspectives on the book's advantages and drawbacks of reading it.

Book reviews enable audiences to talk about their perspective on a book, with a majority of written reviews helping authors and other readers understand the work and help them make purchasing decisions.

Book reviews are written by qualified experts who work for magazines, review websites, scholarly journals, and literature review publications.

Book reviews are generally evaluative and interactive, detailing what a book is about, writing commentaries and assessments about the book through critical feedback, and detailing strengths and weaknesses.

Typically, reviews are brief. In newspapers and academic journals, they rarely exceed 1000 words, although you may encounter lengthier assignments and extended commentaries. In either case, reviews need to be succinct.

CHAPTER TWO

COMPONENTS OF A GOOD REVIEW

A successful book review is expected to include a short summary of the book in review, background information about the author and topic, and an evaluation of the content. When writing a short summary of the book, assume that your audience has not read the book in view and address the book's main topics and ideas and explain their importance.

KEY COMPONENTS OF A GOOD BOOK REVIEW

The key components of a good book review include:

1. Introduction: This provides context for the review, and gives readers a sense of what the book is about. You can include information about the author, the genre, and any relevant historical or cultural context that will help readers understand the book.

2. Summary: The summary section provides a brief overview of the book's plot, characters, and themes. Be careful not to give away spoilers or reveal too much of the story, at the same time making sure to cover the main points.

3. Analysis: This is the heart of the review, where you provide your analysis and evaluation of the book. Always consider the author's style, the structure of the book, the effectiveness of the characters and themes, and any other elements that you feel are important. Use specific examples from the book to support your arguments and try to be as objective as possible.

4. Evaluation: This section provides your overall assessment of the book. Would you recommend it to others? What are its strengths and weaknesses? What did you think of the author's style and approach? Be honest and balanced in your evaluation, and provide evidence to support your arguments.

5. Personal opinion (what it made you feel and think): Although the review should be objective, it's also important to include your personal opinion and response to the book. This can help readers understand why you feel the way you do about the book and can add a more personal touch to the review.

6. Criticism: A good book review should include constructive criticism of the book. This means pointing out areas where you feel the author could have done better or areas where the book fell short of your expectations. However, it's important to be respectful and avoid personal attacks or insults.

7. Comparison: Comparing the book to others in the same genre or on similar topics can be helpful for readers who are trying to decide whether to read the book. This can also help highlight the book's unique qualities and contributions.

8. Target audience: It's important to consider the intended audience for the book and whether it would be a good fit for that audience. For example, a book written for children may be reviewed differently than a book written for adults. Keep in mind who the book is intended for and whether it achieves its intended purpose.

9. Use of Language: A book review should use clear and concise language to convey your thoughts and opinions on the book. Avoid using overly technical language or jargon that may be difficult for readers to understand. Use language that is appropriate for the intended audience and maintain a consistent tone throughout the review.

10. Conclusion: The conclusion should summarize the main points of the review and reiterate your overall assessment of the book. You may also include a final thought or recommendation for readers. Make sure the conclusion is clear and leaves readers with a sense of your opinion of the book.

A good book review therefore, should provide readers with a clear and unbiased evaluation of the book. It should include a brief summary, an analysis of the book's strengths and weaknesses, and a personal opinion. By including these key elements, you can provide readers with valuable insight into whether the book is worth their time and money.

Summarily, a review should include:

- The name of the author and the book title and the main theme.
- Relevant details about who the author is and where he/she stands in the genre or field of inquiry.
- The context of the book and/or your review.
- The thesis of the book.
- Your thesis about the book.

CHAPTER THREE

READING FOR COMPREHENSION

In book review, there are a range of basic skills which a reviewer needs to possess in order to produce top notch reviews. One of such is Reading and comprehension skills. Reading and understanding the book prior to the reviewing task is critical to having a good review. A reviewer who lacks an understanding of the book will definitely produce a poor review.

Reading for comprehension is the ability to comprehend or understand, what you are reading. It is the ability to process written text, understand its meaning, and to integrate it with what the reader already knows. Reading Comprehension is the ability to easily and efficiently read the text for meaning. This is an intentional and active part of reading and takes place before, during and after you read something. By being able to comprehend what you are reading, you can extract meaning from the text and better realize what the author is trying to convey.

There are two components of reading for comprehension:
    a. Text comprehension and
    b. Vocabulary knowledge.

Vocabulary knowledge is the ability to understand the language being used, while text comprehension is using this language to develop an awareness of what the meaning is behind the text.

Strategies To Improve Reading Comprehension Skills.

There are several reading strategies that you can begin implementing today to improve your reading comprehension skills. The more you practice, the better you will become at understanding what you are reading. The following are seven simple strategies you can use to work on your comprehension skills

1. Improve your vocabulary: Knowing what the words you are reading mean can improve your ability to comprehend the meaning of the text.

2. Come up with questions about the text you are reading: Asking questions about what you are reading can help improve your reading comprehension by allowing you to become invested in the text. It can also broaden your overall understanding of what you are reading by enabling you to explore themes, motifs and other components of text that you otherwise wouldn't inquire about.

3. Use context clues: Using context clues is a great way to understand what you are reading even if you don't know all the vocabulary being used. Context clues can be found in the words and sentences surrounding the word that you aren't familiar with. To use context clues, you can focus on the key phrases or ideas in a sentence and deduce the main idea of a sentence or paragraph based on this information. You can also look for nearby words that are synonyms or antonyms of the word you don't know.

4. Look for the main idea: Identifying the main idea of a paragraph or article can help you determine the importance of the article. Understanding why what you're reading is important can give you a better comprehension of what the author is trying to convey. When reading, pause every few paragraphs and see if you can decipher what the main idea is. Then, try to put the main idea in your own words for even further understanding.

5. Write a summary of what you read: A great way to increase your knowledge of what you have read is to write a summary. Summarizing requires you to decide what is important in the text and then put it in your own words. Summarizing allows you to

determine if you truly understand what you have read and better remember what you have read in the long term. The written summaries should include only relevant details. The summaries must reflect that you understood the text. Use your own words as much as possible as this shows that you understood the text.

6. While a reviewer may aptly take excerpts from a text to drive home a point, incessant and mindless lifting of whole sections or paragraphs in text for summaries suggest poor understanding of a text.

7. Break up the reading into smaller sections: If you are reading longer or more challenging text, consider breaking it up into smaller sections. For example, you could read two paragraphs at a time and then pause to quickly summarize what you just read in your mind. Breaking up what you are reading can help you feel less overwhelmed and give you a better chance of truly comprehending the information in the text.

8. Pace yourself: Pacing yourself is also an effective way to work on your reading comprehension skills by allowing you to set realistic goals for your reading practice and habits. This is especially true for books or other literature that you find challenging. Set a goal for yourself that you know you can meet each day. For example, rather than saying that you want to read an entire book in two days, say that you will read three chapters a night. This allows you to reach your goals and also provides adequate time for you to process what you are reading between each session.

Tips to make the most of your reading comprehension practice

Reading is a fundamental part of everyday life. The more you incorporate and prioritize reading and understanding what you read, the better your overall reading comprehension will become. These tips can help you make the most of your time when practicing your reading skills.

- Eliminate distractions: When you are distracted, your ability to comprehend what you are reading is negatively impacted. When reading—even if it's a simple email—eliminate distractions and focus solely on the text. This will help you learn to hold your attention to what you read and enable you to know whether you understand what you are reading.

- Read a book below your reading level: Starting with books below your reading level will allow you to develop a baseline of your reading comprehension and build on that. Instead of starting with books or other text that you find challenging, read something that is comfortable and that you can easily comprehend.

- Re-read text to ensure understanding: If you finish a sentence or paragraph and realize that you don't understand what it was trying to convey, take the time to re-read it until you do. Try to read more slowly the second time around and look up definitions for any words you don't know the meaning of.

- Read aloud: Reading aloud incorporates both visual and audio learning into your reading comprehension practice. It also forces you to slow down and gives you more time to process what you are reading.

The Different Levels of Comprehension.

1. Lexical Comprehension

Characteristics:
- It deals with the understanding of the words in a text.
- The reader must be equipped with the knowledge of unlocking the meaning of the terms in a text.

2. Literal Comprehension

Characteristics:
- Identify the main ideas of the paragraph.
- Recall details to support the main idea.
- Organize the sequence of main events that occurred.

3. Interpretive Comprehension

Characteristics:
- Reading between the lines.
- Predict endings and anticipate consequences.
- State reasons for events.
- Make generalizations.
- Understand the facts that are explicitly stated in the text.

4. Applied Comprehension

Characteristics:
- Reading beyond the lines.
- Reader links between the text and his own experience and knowledge to develop an answer.
- A reader asks open-ended questions to promote deeper understanding.
- Readers support their answer with a logical reason.
- Readers do the following:
- Make generalizations.
- Make comparisons.
- Make judgments.
- Make recommendations and suggestions.
- Make decisions.
- Create alternative endings.

5. Affective Comprehension

Characteristics:
- Previews social scripts to ensure understanding of plot development.
- Connects motive to plot and character development.

CHAPTER FOUR
How To Identify Key Points In Book Review

➤ **Read the book & take notes.** If possible, read it many times, repeat reads tends to bring better view aspects of the book setting and, character in a new way.
- Write down notes in a notebook/use a voice recorder.
- Summarize the major sections of the book for better understanding of its structures.

➤ **Think about the book's genre and / or field of study.**
- Consider how the book fits/does not fit in its genre/field of study.

➤ **Determine the major arguments & themes of the book.**
- The theme is often a lesson/overall message that the reader perceives between the lines.
- The theme may be the fundamental and often universal ideas explored in a book
- There may be multiple themes especially works of friction.
- The theme help support the argument that the book is making.
- Stretch the one-word summary you discovered about the book into a sentence.

➤ **Consider the author's writing style.**
- Check whether the style suits the intended audience
- Check if it is genre (a category of writing) or style (manner in which a subject is expressed/performed)

➤ **Check the development of the major areas/points in the book**
- Areas covered
- Areas not covered
- Locate gaps

- **Note the book's format**
  - the book layout, typography etc (provides framing/context for the book)
  - Check secondary materials (maps, charts and drawings) and how they support/contribute to the book's themes and arguments
- **Check any literary devices in the book**
  - Take note of the book's-- character/plot/setting/symbols/mood/tone and how these are related to the overall theme of the book.
- **Check the uniqueness of the book**
  - Any new information to a genre?
  - Is any existing rules or norms challenged/expanded?
  - If yes, how was that done?
  - How will this affect the intended audience's reception of the book?
- **Check how successful the book is**
  - Is there success of overall purpose of the book?
  - Is the conclusion satisfactory?
  - Can you recommend the book?

Methodology

- **Begin with a heading**
  - Bibliographic information
  - title
  - Author
  - Place of publication
  - Publisher
  - Date of publication
  - Number of pages
- **Write an introduction**
  - Good introduction grabs the reader's attention and their interest in reading the entire review and set the tone for the whole review.

- Must contain relevant details (the author's background and possible previous work in the genre)
- Indicate main theme to be discussed
- Possible inclusion in the introduction is; historical moment/ surprising or intriguing statement.
- A times, introduction can be written last when unsure from the beginning. The supporting points gained while going through the book helps develop good introduction. This helps the introduction to match the book content.

➤ **Write book summary**
- Summary should be short, concise and informative
- Summary can be supported by proper quotes/ paraphrasing from the book. Avoid plagiarism
- Summary should capture the book's setting/ narrative voice/ critical analysis
- Summary should not be too wordy
- Summary must not omit important details.

➤ **Evaluate and critique the book**
- Be direct and clear
- Property formulated critique
- Book's goal achievement should be addressed
- Compare the book to other books on the subject
- Address unconvincing specific points, not properly developed
- Use properly cited quotes from the book to back up your critique. This provides reinforcement and trustworthy source

CHAPTER FIVE

SUMMARY WRITING

What Is A Summary?

Summary is a collection of paraphrases from an original text (a shorter version) which can be one-fourth to one-tenth of the original text in paraphrases (Deanza.edu, 2023). It is a concise overview of the original text in one's own words by providing an accurate account of an original text without losing information that is being passed across to the audience (McCombes, 2023).

Summary is also identifying the most important information in a text and stating them in one's own words (kellog.edu). summaries are used to prepare the readers for an analysis of the test (i.e., review) as it is done to review the main themes in a text (Study.com, 2023).

There are different reasons for writing summaries which depend on the class of people involved; for instance, students need summaries to learn about new information, take research notes, and so on. In the same vein, scholars also sometimes refer to summaries as an abstract i.e., a text that makes the content of a long article known to its readers prior reading the entire text (LLCC Writing Center, 2021).

Characteristics Of A Good Summary

- A good summary should give an understanding of the text being summarized.
- A good summary should be short, unbiased and flow well.
- A good summary should focus on what the writer says not

what he or she does or how well it is done.

- A good summary does not judge the idea of the writer (except it is an evaluative/critical summary).
- A good summary should only include what is found in the text being summarized and nothing outside the text.

Steps To Writing A Good Summary (Mccombes, 2023)

1. Read the text: scan, read and skim the text. Scanning is reading a text quickly to get a general understanding of the content; reading entails highlighting important points in the text and skimming involves re-reading through the text to ensure everything is properly understood (scribbr.com).

2. Break the text into sections e.g., introduction, methods, results, conclusion.

3. Identify key points in each section of the text although not all paragraphs of the text should be paraphrased; paraphrase only the essential points.

4. Write the summary by paraphrasing the author's idea properly, avoiding plagiarism by not copying the exact text.

5. Cite the source of the summary being written.

6. Check the summary with the full text to avoid paraphrasing using similar words. Plagiarism checker can be useful.

CHAPTER SIX

COMMON GRAMMATICAL ERRORS

Grammatical Errors And Book Review

A book reviewer should be conversant with errors of grammar in order to offer the required feedback for any author to improve in this area of his work. Some of the errors writers make in their writing include but are not limited to the following:

The omission of an essential sentence elements such as Subject, Predicator, complement.

1. Omission of subject e.g.,' I am going to be available' not '...am going to be available

2. Wrong use of modal operators e.g., may/might, can/could. Modal verbs do not need a preposition after them except '' ought to". All other modal verbs are followed by the base form of verbs.' I must + go 'not 'I must + to go'.

3. Misuse or omission of articles – Articles A, An and The are sometimes misused or entirely omitted in sentences where they are supposed to be used e.g.,

    i   Do not make a noise not 'do not make noise'.

    ii   I bought a broom not 'I bought broom'

4. Confusion or ambiguity in the use of pronouns – When pronouns are used to make reference in sentences, the referent must be clear to avoid ambiguity e.g., The man gave John his car which he had left in his care. (It is not clear whose car is referred to in the sentence and who had left the car in whose car. This kind of sentence confuses the reader and authors would do well to use

clearer referents in sentences.

5. Misuse of countable and uncountable nouns – This is a common error which authors should equally avoid. Using 'much' in place of 'many' is common e.g., The boys in the school are much. 'Boys' in this sentence is countable and so it should have been 'many boys. I do not want to carry much books should also be: I do not want to carry many books (book is a countable noun)

6. Wrong use of Prepositions – Prepositions in the English Language collocate with other words in certain ways and good writers are expected to be conversant with these forms. Examples of prepositions and how they collocate with other words are shown below: in danger, out of reach, on foot (not by foot), arrive at, concentrate on, in transit etc. Collocations are somewhat fixed in English and consciously mastering them enhances accuracy in the language.

7. Misuse of relatives, subordinators and conjunctions – A mastery of the use of relative Pronouns (who, which, whose, that and whom) and subordinating conjunctions in sentences is required for error free writings. Consider these examples:

    i   This is the woman whose bag was stolen.

    ii   This is the woman to whom I gave some money. This is the woman who left her shoes in my car (Note that 'whose' shows possession, 'who' is used to refer to the subject and 'whom' refers to object)

8. Errors in concord- Concord simply means that the subject in a sentence must agree with the verb in number and tense i.e., singular Nouns take singular verbs and the tenses in a sentence must be consistent. Some errors of concord are shown below:

    i   The girls reads in the hostel (wrong), The girls read in the hostel(right)

    ii   The girl read in the hostel (wrong), The girl reads in the hostel

    iii   They knows what they are doing (wrong), They know what they are doing (right)

iv She see me everyday (Wrong), She sees me every day (right)

Note that unlike nouns, when we add 's' to a verb, it becomes singular

9. Misrelated or dangling participles– Participles are forms of verbs used in other positions apart from the verbal position. They are usually in the progressive form eg driving, running, feeding etc

i Driving furiously, the pet was hit inadvertently. (It is not clear here, who was driving clearly)

ii Driving furiously, The drunk driver hit the pet (The missing subject is included).

Dangling participles are those that are not placed close to the nouns they modify thereby making the sentence vague. Like adjectives, participles must have a noun to modify or else they will be hanging.

10. Misuse of intransitive and transitive verbs – Transitive verbs are verbs that take objects in sentences. The way to know them is to locate the verb in the sentence and try fixing a noun or noun phrase after it e.g.

i The chef cooked the food that we ate (cooked is a transitive verb)

ii The Chef cooked (this is incomplete and unacceptable in standard English)

iii We won the gold (We Won …)

11. Misuse of active and passive voices – Errors can also arise from the misuse of active and passive voice e.g.

i The labourers are building the house (Active); The house is being built (passive)

ii The man bought a house (Active); A house was bought by him (passive)

The most common error that is made when using active/passive voice is inability to use the correct form of verbs. In order to make a sentence passive, the past form of verb 'to be' and the 'past

participle' form of the main verb are used. Common errors arise from:
- a Using the wrong tense e.g., 'being' and 'been'. Consider:
  - i We are being corrected for our misbehavior (correct);
  - ii We are been corrected for our misbehavior (wrong).
- b Leaving out the object in active voice.

12. Errors in comparative constructions - These kinds of errors are also common with authors. An example is using the comparative form in place of superlative or vice versa.
   - i The girl is the neater person in her room (wrong)
   - ii The girl is the neatest person in her room (right)

13. Errors also arise when writers use '-er' with 'more' e.g.
   - i I am more happier when I have more money (wrong)
   - ii I am happier when I have more money (Right).

Note that when referring to one item the non- comparative form is used e.g., The lady is pretty. When comparing two items we use the comparative form e.g., She is prettier than her friend. She is the prettiest of all the girls.

A good book is one that is free of errors, grammatical and otherwise. In order for a book to be highly rated and attract quality readership, the author would need to engage the services of professional editors and book reviewers to go through the manuscript and make necessary corrections before publishing. Books that are ridden with errors would definitely attract poor sales.

CHAPTER SEVEN

CRITICAL THINKING AND EVALUATION

Introduction

Thoughts are expressed in different ways. One fundamental way of expressing thoughts is the language which may be written or oral. The advent of western education has created a giant monument in thought expression through writing. The things expressed in writing represent the flow of thoughts of the writer.

Some writers are cohesive in their thoughts and this reflects in the symmetry of presentation. Others are not so cohesive; ideas are disjointed and you have to fish out the basic things expressed that may not appear too obvious. The style of writing is another thing. Some use suspense; some are dramatic and some others express thoughts in sequence. The third factor has to do with language use. Some use simple, easy to understand language while some are complex in language use and presentation. For instance, T.M Aluko's writings are in simple prose while that of Wole Soyinka is somehow complex. The command of language depends on the author's linguistic prowess and also determined by the audience being addressed. Style can be simple, flowery or elegant. All these will have effect on how we are to receive the thoughts expressed in the writings.

It is not possible for every reader to have a physical contact with the writer of a given material. At the same time, we want to sit in our corner to look closely at what is written and unravel the real intentions of the writer. Part of comprehension is the ability to understand the thoughts expressed. This is where critical thinking comes in.

Synonyms for critical thinking include brainstorming, conceptualizing, deliberating, inventing, problem solving, reasoning, thinking, abstract thought and consideration.

What Is Critical Thinking?

The term critical comes from the Greek word kritikos meaning "able to judge or discern". Critical thinking is the objective analysis and evaluation of an issue in order to form a judgement.

"Critical thinking is a kind of thinking in which you question, analyse, interpret, evaluate and make a judgement about what you read, hear, say, or write."

The root of critical thinking could be found in logic as expressed in the era of Socrates and Plato, two foremost philosophers of the early age, but the term critical thinking was first coined by an American philosopher, John Dewey, in his book "How We Think" (1910). The coinage was later adopted by the progressive education movement as a core instructional goal that offered a dynamic modern alternative to the traditional educational method of rote memorization.

Let's consider some tit-bits from Wikipedia:

"Critical thinking is the analysis of available facts, evidence, observations, and arguments in order to form a judgement by the application of rational, sceptical, and unbiased analyses and evaluation.[1] The application of critical thinking includes self-directed, self-disciplined, self-monitored, and self-corrective habits of mind,[2] thus a critical thinker is a person who practices the skills of critical thinking or has been trained and educated in its disciplines.[3] Richard W. Paul said that the mind of a critical thinker engages the person's intellectual abilities and personality traits.[4] Critical thinking presupposes assent to rigorous standards of excellence and mindful command of their use in effective communication and problem solving, and a commitment to overcome egocentrism and sociocentrism.[5][6]

(Wikipedia)"

In a nutshell, critical thinking is the process whereby the intellectual capacity of the reader is brought to bear on the author's presentation to attain better understanding.

Critical Thinking Skills

There are seven critical thinking skills and these are:
1. Analysis - this is the ability to dissect the various thoughts expressed in the writing.
2. Interpretation - some writings do not have obvious meanings. The reader should decode the meanings as a way of aiding comprehension.
3. Inference - this is the ability to discern the likely thoughts of the writer that are not obviously expressed.
4. Explanation - this is the ability to explain in simple terms what is read and the perceived intents of the writer.
5. Self-Regulation - the reader should regulate his thoughts to make sure that the basic thoughts of the writer are not coloured by personal experiences and prejudices. For instance, Wole Soyinka is a traditionalist. A Christian who wants to understand his writings will have regulate himself in the area of profession of faith.
6. Open-mindedness - this is the ability to open one's mind to new concepts and ideas without being extremely judgmental.
7. Problem solving - this is the ability to find answers to series of questions and challenges that the writing may present.

How To Do Critical Thinking

Critical thinking occurs when readers analyse, evaluate, interpret or synthesize information and apply creative thought to form an argument, solve a problem, or reach a conclusion. Although critical thinking process differ between individuals but there are some useful steps to follow:
1. Identification of the problematic issues at hand and the cause.

2. Analysis of the various arguments.
3. Discovery of the basic and underlining facts.
4. Challenge of personal biases so that they do not creep into the appraisal.
5. Decide on the perceived significance.
6. Arriving at conclusions.

Pillars Of Critical Thinking

What helps thinking is the understanding of the subject matter being considered. Comprehension of the writing is a major key here. To help understanding, the reader makes inferences where needed, makes direct observations in some cases, generalize in some instances, abridge his biases and finally draw his conclusion. There are four pillars that would help critical thinking:

- Analysis - College graduates are used to this type of question.
- Interpretation - Interpretation is related to analysis.
- Evaluation - The real word is all about results.
- Self-Direction - Figuring out what to do next sounds like an obvious skill, but it is amazing that so many people lack this skill.

What Are The Tools Of Critical Thinking?

These include the following: inference and direct observation; generalization and overgeneralisation; premise and conclusion; bias and point of view. Students cannot think deeply about a topic if they know little about it.

The Main Purpose Of Critical Thinking And Benefits:

Critical thinking is aimed at achieving the best possible outcomes in any situation. In order to achieve this, it must involve gathering and evaluating information from as many different sources as possible.

The Benefits Of Critical Thinking Include The Following:

1. It helps to improve decision making.
2. It enhances problem-solving ability.
3. It refines research skills.
4. It polishes the writer's creativity.
5. It stimulates curiosity.

Conclusion: Critical thinking is the analysis of available facts, evidence, observations, and arguments in order to form a judgement by the application of rational, sceptical, and unbiased analyses and evaluation. A well-developed set of Critical Thinking skills builds self-empowerment and confidence. It enables you to efficiently gather knowledge, quickly process information, and intelligently analyse data.

CHAPTER EIGHT

MAJOR PARTS OF A BOOK REVIEW

1. Meaning Of Book Review

Definition: A book review is a critical analysis and evaluation of a literary work that provides readers with an overview of the book's content, style, and its merits or shortcomings.

Purpose: The main purpose of a book review is to inform potential readers about the book's quality, relevance, and potential appeal.

2. Types Of Book Review

- Literary Criticism Review: Focuses on examining the book's literary elements, such as themes, character development, and writing style.
- Academic Review: Written for scholarly purposes, it evaluates a book's contribution to a specific field of study or knowledge.
- Consumer Review: Aimed at informing potential readers about a book's entertainment value, readability, and overall enjoyment factor.

3. Importance Of Book Review

- Guidance for Readers: Book reviews help readers make informed choices by providing insight into the book's strengths and weaknesses.
- Promotes Writers: Positive book reviews can boost an author's reputation and increase book sales.
- Engages Literary Community: Book reviews foster discussions among readers, writers, and academics, contributing to the wider literary community.

4. Features Of Book Review

- Summary: A brief overview of the book's plot or main argument without giving away major spoilers.
- Analysis: Evaluation of the book's strengths and weaknesses, including character development, plot structure, writing style, and overall impact.
- Personal Opinion: The reviewer's subjective opinion and impression of the book, backed by evidence from the text.
- Recommendation: Suggesting who might enjoy the book and in what context it is best suited.

5. Step-By-Step Guide To Review A Book:

- Read the Book: Start by thoroughly reading the book, taking notes on key plot points, characters, and notable quotes.
- Analyze and Evaluate: Consider various aspects of the book, including the writing style, plot structure, character development, and themes.
- Organize Thoughts: Create an outline or structure for your review, deciding what key points you want to cover.
- Write the Review: Begin writing your book review, starting with a captivating introduction, followed by the body paragraphs with your analysis, and concluding with a thoughtful summary.
- Edit and Proofread: Review your work for clarity, coherence, and grammar errors. Ensure your review accurately reflects your thoughts and opinions.

6. Elements Of Book Review:

- Introduction: Provide a brief overview of the book, its author, and the genre or field it belongs to.
- Synopsis: Summarize the book's main plot or argument, highlighting its key aspects.
- Analysis: Critically evaluate the book's strengths and weaknesses, discussing aspects like character development, writing style, and plot.
- Comparison: If relevant, compare the book to similar works

or other works by the same author.

- Conclusion: Offer a concise summary of your overall assessment, including your recommendation to potential readers.

7. Additional Elements

- Historical/Contextual Analysis: Explore how the book fits within the historical or cultural context it was written in.
- Social or Political Relevance: Discuss how the book addresses or reflects societal issues and the impact it may have.
- Literary Techniques: Analyse the author's use of literary devices, such as metaphor, symbolism, or foreshadowing, and its effectiveness.

CHAPTER NINE

BENEFITS OF A BOOK REVIEW

Introduction

Book reviews are an integral part of the literary world, serving as valuable tools that offer various advantages to readers, authors, and the broader literary community. This detailed write-up explores the key benefits of book reviews, highlighting their impact on fostering literary appreciation, encouraging critical thinking, and supporting author development.

Benefits Of Book Review

The Benefits of Book Review: Fostering Literary Appreciation, Critical Thinking, and Author Development

1. Literary Appreciation: Book reviews play a vital role in promoting literary appreciation among readers. They expose readers to a wide range of literary works, genres, and authors, encouraging them to explore beyond their comfort zones. By providing insights into the themes and writing style of a book, reviews help readers make informed choices about their reading selections. (Source: National Endowment for the Arts, "Reading at Risk: A Survey of Literary Reading in America.")

2. Stimulating Critical Thinking: Book reviews stimulate critical thinking and intellectual engagement. They present varying perspectives and interpretations of a book, prompting readers to consider different viewpoints and evaluate the merits of the arguments presented. This critical analysis enhances readers' cognitive abilities and enriches their reading experience. (Source: Rosentrater, C. L., & Williams, T. L. "The Role of Book

Reviews in Intellectual Discourse.")

3. **Author Recognition and Exposure:** Book reviews are essential for authors seeking recognition and exposure in the literary world. Positive reviews can create buzz around a book, leading to increased visibility and potential new readership. This exposure is especially crucial for new and emerging authors looking to establish their presence in the competitive publishing landscape. (Source: Charness, G., Gneezy, U., & Kuhn, M. A. "Experimental Methods: Between-subject and Within-subject Design.")

4. **Constructive Feedback and Growth:** Book reviews provide authors with constructive feedback on their work. While positive reviews offer encouragement, critical reviews can offer valuable insights into areas that may need improvement. Authors can use this feedback to refine their writing style, strengthen their storytelling, and grow as writers. (Source: Fry, R. "Making the Writing Process Work: Strategies for Composition and Self-Regulation.")

5. **Influence on Book Sales:** Book reviews have a significant impact on book sales. Studies have shown that books with positive reviews and higher ratings tend to sell better than those with fewer or negative reviews. Positive reviews create a sense of trust among potential readers, leading to higher chances of book purchases. (Source: Chevalier, J. A., & Mayzlin, D. "The Effect of Word of Mouth on Sales: Online Book Reviews.")

Conclusion

Book reviews are not only helpful tools for readers seeking literary recommendations but also serve as crucial platforms for authors to gain recognition and grow in their writing journey. By fostering literary appreciation, stimulating critical thinking, and offering constructive feedback, book reviews contribute significantly to the overall enrichment of the literary community. Embracing and supporting the culture of book reviews can lead to a more vibrant and dynamic literary landscape, benefiting readers and authors alike.

REFERENCE

- Christopher Taylor(2023). How to write a Book Review. August 6 www.wikihow.com
- Denza.edu (2023). Summary Writing retrieved from https://www.deanza.edu/esl/documents/Summary%20Writing.pdf on 4th August, 2023
- LLCC Writing Center (2021). Writing a good summary retrieved from https://www.llcc.edu/sites/default/files/2021-11/Writing%20a%20Summary.pdf on 4th August, 2023.
- Masterclass.com (2023). How to write a summary: 4 Tips for Writing a Good Summary-2023 retrieved from https://www.masterclass.com/articles/how-to-write-a-summary on 1st August, 2023.
- McCombes, S. (2023, May 31). How to Write a Summary | Guide & Examples. Scribbr. Retrieved August 4, 2023, from https://www.scribbr.com/working-with-sources/how-to-summarize/Study.com, (2023). Summary Definition, Types & Examples retrieved from https://study.com/learn/lesson/what-is-a-summary.html on 1st August, 2023.
- John Dewey (1910) - How We Think
- Wikipedia - https://en-wikipedia.org
- w.w.w.kialo-edu.com - Critical Thinking Skills.
- w.w.w.criticalthinking.org - Defining Critical Thinking

Printed in the USA
CPSIA information can be obtained
at www.ICGtesting.com
LVHW010907260224
772821LV00003B/164